THE SIERRA LEONE GOVERNMENT RAILWAY
FROM CREATION TO PRESERVATION

by Helen Ashby

Published by Mainline & Maritime Ltd, 3 Broadleaze, Upper Seagry, near Chippenham, SN15 5EY
Tel: 07770 748615 www.mainlineandmaritime.co.uk orders@mainlineandmaritime.co.uk
Printed in the UK

ISBN: 978-1-900340-75-5 © Mainline & Maritime Ltd, & Contributors 2020

Front Cover: As the Sierra Leone Railway was preparing for closure, the Welshpool & Llanfair Railway in mid-Wales was seeking to expand its locomotive and rolling stock fleet. On hearing that a 2ft 6in gauge railway in West Africa was scrapping all its equipment, the late Pasco Rowe and colleagues took a trip to Sierra Leone to identify whether any suitable material could be acquired.

Hunslet 2-6-2 Tank locomotive SLR No 85 was demonstrated for them in steam at Fisher Lane Depot in April 1975 and a deal was struck to bring the locomotive to Wales.

Pasco Rowe Collection, Sierra Leone National Railway Museum

Above: A passenger train stands at Moyamba Station, c1905. The line opened to Moyamba in October 1900, bringing the length of operating railway to 75¾ miles. Regular local services began operation with one train per day from Freetown. The single fare from Freetown to Moyamba was 4s/6d. and the return fare was 7s/5d. The journey time between Freetown and Moyamba was six hours.

David Swift Collection, Sierra Leone National Railway Museum

Back Cover: No 151 is seen entering yard at Bauya Junction, hauling a branch-line train, c1928.

F.A.J.Utting MA, MEd (1905-1989) Lecturer Fourah Bay College 1927-30.
Photographs donated to the Sierra Leone National Railway Museum by Joyce Chamberlain and Stanley Utting

INTRODUCTION

2020 has been a difficult year for all of us, wherever we are, as the novel coronavirus pandemic has swept through the world. The tourist industry has been particularly hard hit, with travel disrupted, international borders closed and visitor attractions closed for the duration.

The Friends of the Sierra Leone National Railway Museum has continued to support the museum throughout the crisis, since visitors are few and the Sierra Leone Government has struggled to manage the national economy. However, we have been unable to hold any of our usual fundraising events and have sought other means of maintaining contact with members and raising funds to help our colleagues in West Africa. This means that we are doubly grateful to Iain McCall and Mainline & Maritime for their generosity in enabling this book and for their kind support for the museum and its Friends.

Publications relating to the Sierra Leone Railway are few and far between, and high-quality images of the railway in operation are scarce, so much was destroyed during the ten years of civil unrest in Sierra Leone in the 1990s. I would like to thank all of those who have kindly donated photographs to the museum, or simply lent them for use in this book and for your permission to share them – without you this publication would not have been possible and the museum would be the poorer for it.

Where possible I have tried to select material that has not previously been published. I can only apologise for the quality of many of the images, where the originals are in poor condition or were of low quality when taken. It is important to recognise that few are the work of professional or semi-professional photographers, but were snaps taken to preserve the memory of something special that has now disappeared.

Particular thanks are due to William Bickers-Jones and Steve Davies MBE for kindly agreeing to prof-read the book for me and for ensuring that it does not include too many grammatical, political or historical blunders.

Helen Ashby OBE
Chair, Friends of the Sierra Leone National Railway Museum
Author/Compiler

The Freetown terminus of the Sierra Leone Railway was at Water Street. The station, close to the Government Wharf. The station was served by extensive goods sidings, from whence the goods train in the picture is heading towards the station and which can be seen in the background to the left of this picture, taken c1907.

David Swift Collection, Sierra Leone National Railway Museum

3

A BRIEF HISTORY OF THE SIERRA LEONE RAILWAY

There were several proposals for a railway from 1874 onwards, including an early proposal for a trans-Saharan Railway, but none came to anything until 1893, when a scheme backed by the Liverpool Chamber of Commerce obtained approval from the Colonial Government.

William Shelford & Sons were appointed as surveyors for the new railway, alongside proposed routes in Gold Coast (now Ghana) and Lagos (Nigeria). Surveying was completed and construction started in 1896.

The gauge chosen was 2ft 6in, partly to keep the costs to a minimum – smaller is cheaper – but also to cope with rough terrain and because it was small enough to make in the UK and ship as a kit of parts.

Construction started on the site of a disused racecourse in Cline Town, at the eastern end of Freetown, where there was ample space for storing all the necessary materials and equipment on a site close to the deep water quay, where all the material imported from the UK would be landed.

Construction took place both eastwards towards the Liberian border and westwards through the city towards the eventual terminus at Water Street.

The railway reached its eastern terminus at Pendembu, 227 miles from Water Street, and was officially taken over from the contractors on 1st August 1908.

In addition, a branch northward was built between 1914 and 1916 from Bauya Junction to Makeni and Kamabai, with a length of 104 miles, bringing the total route mileage to 331 miles though the branch was cut back to Makeni in 1930.

The railway continued in operation under the Colonial government until 1961, when Sierra Leone gained independence from Britain, and was then handed over for the new government to operate.

A further line of 5 and a half miles was built in 1903, known as the Mountain Railway, which enabled Europeans to leave the mosquito infested city and move up the hill to the more rarefied air towards Leicester Peak. The advent of motor cars and buses quickly superseded this railway and it was closed in 1929.

There were few years during its history when the Sierra Leone Railway made any profit from its operations, but it provided a valuable service to the government, to the population and to business and agriculture, opening up the links between the interior, the capital, the sea and therefore the rest of the world. It was especially important to the war effort during WW2.

However, post-Independence in the 1960s the Sierra Leone Railway was proving a headache to the Sierra Leone Government, depending on ever mounting subsidies to sustain its existence. The railway infrastructure needed refurbishment and the railway was found to be inefficient and non-profitable. A decline in traffic on the railway and an increasing emphasis on road traffic led to a significant change in Government Policy

The General Manager at the time, Solomon A J Pratt, undertook research to identify ways to make the railway more profitable. He claimed that all the studies undertaken during his term of Office as General Manager of the Sierra Leone Railway underscored the necessity for the continuance and improvement of the Railway – he understood the benefits of the railway to the wider economy rather than seeing it as a profit-making concern. The resulting recommendation was for the continuance of and improvement to the railway, including a new branch to serve a bauxite mine, and conversion to a wider gauge.

A request was made to the World Bank for an infrastructure loan, but the request was rejected with a recommendation to close the railway and improve the road infrastructure and the phasing out of the railway began in 1967.

The Makeni Branch closed in 1968. After that the railway closed gradually starting from Pendembu and working back westwards towards Freetown. The last official passenger train operated on the SLR on 17th November 1974, hauled by Beyer Garratt Locomotive No 73, which is now preserved in the Sierra Leone National Railway Museum. Trains ran on a sporadic basis until mid-1975 up as far as Bauya Junction but the final lifting of track in August 1975 put an end to this.

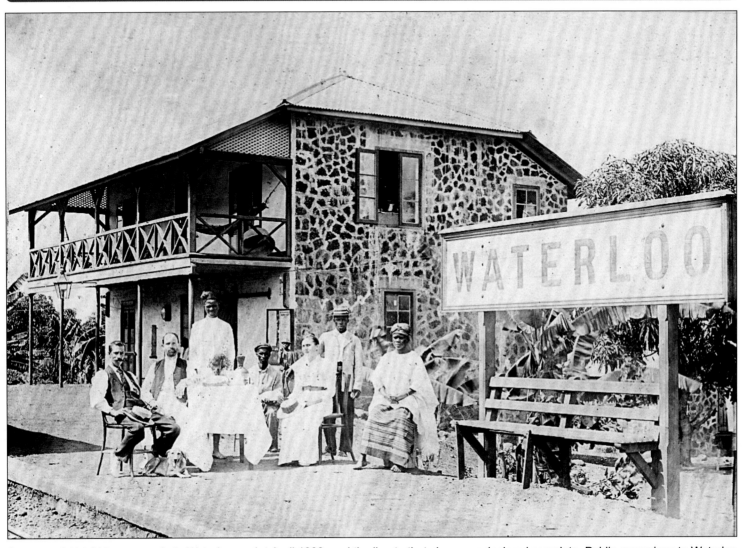

A successful trial trip was made to Waterloo on 1st April 1898, and the line to that place was declared complete. Public excursions to Waterloo were run on Good Friday and Easter Monday, April 8th and 11th, and in October a regular Saturday service between Freetown, Kissy, Wellington, Hastings and Waterloo was inaugurated. Pictured here is Benjamin Armes (on the left), Locomotive Superintendent to the Sierrra Leone Government Railway from 1897 to 1904, pictured with his wife and the station staff at Waterloo.

From the collection of Julia West

Above The Sierra Leone Railway was officially opened at 8 am on 1st May 1899, by the Acting Governor of Sierra Leone, His Excellency Major M Nathan RE CMG at Water Street Station Freetown. The day was declared a public holiday and according to the official history of the railway, written in 1949 to celebrate its 50th anniversary, by Chief Mechanical Engineer J Ralph Best:

"Freetown was beflagged for the occasion, the new station buildings being particularly conspicuous. The streets outside were lined with police and the band of the West Indian Regiment was in attendance. Railway employees wearing blue uniforms relieved by green stripes on legs, sleeves and neck and with brass buttons, were on duty inside the station."

The National Archives of Sierra Leone

Left Locomotive Superintendent Benjamin Armes and his wife, taking a trip along the new line on a track inspection trolley. Benjamin Armes was employed by the Crown Agents and consulting engineers Messrs Shelford, as the Locomotive Superintendent, in charge of maintaining the engines on the railway, then under construction. His salary was £50 per annum (equivalent to approximately £28,000 in 2015).

From the collection of Julia West

Locomotive Superintendent Benjamin Armes takes the Acting Governor Major Sir Matthew Nathan (centre) on a visit to inspect the railway, 1899.

From the collection of Julia West

This picture depicts the first train crossing the river Taia bridge near Mano after testing on the 3rd September 1902. The bridge was 589 feet long and of ten spans.

From the collection of Julia West

This fine six span viaduct crossed the Orogu River at mile 11 over a very bad piece of land with rocks and water hidden under the dense growth of shrub. It is 386 feet long and built on concrete and steel trestles on a tight radius of only 5 chains (330 feet). The lady in the photograph is Mathilda Armes, wife of the Locomotive Superintendent, c1900.

From the collection of Julia West

The line opened as far as Baiima in 1905, by which time a new Engineer, Edward Willoughby had taken up the supervision of construction. Mr Willoughby is depicted here with a construction train, headed by SLGR No 3 Bai Bureh, an 0-4-0 Saddle Tank built by W G Bagnall of Stafford in 1898.

David Swift Collection, Sierra Leone National Railway Museum

The rainy season in Sierra Leone starts around the beginning of May and lasts until October every year. The heavy rains often caused problems for the railway infrastructure though landslips and washing away of embankments. In this picture, Engineer Edward Willoughby and his team are surveying the effects of a storm at Kissy, just to the east of Freetown, in September 1906.

David Swift Collection, Sierra Leone National Railway Museum

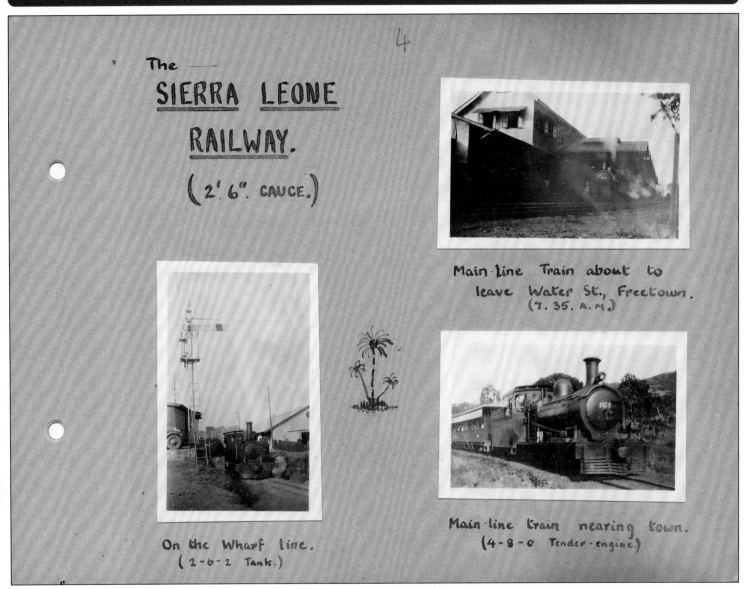

4

The
SIERRA LEONE
RAILWAY.
(2' 6". GAUGE.)

Main-line Train about to leave Water St, Freetown. (7. 35. A.M.)

On the Wharf line. (2-6-2 Tank.)

Main-line train nearing town. (4-8-0 Tender-engine.)

F A J Utting MA, Med went to Sierra Leone in 1927 to lecture in history at Fourah Bay College, where he remained until 1930. During those three years he photographed many aspects of life in the country and compiled a delightful album, which he subsequently used to inform his book 'The Story of Sierra Leone' published in 1931 as a text for students and teachers. Three pages of the album are devoted to images of the Sierra Leone Government Railway in action.

F.A.J.Utting MA, MEd (1905-1989) Lecturer Fourah Bay College 1927-30.
Photographs donated to the Sierra Leone National Railway Museum by Joyce Chamberlain and Stanley Utting

Sierra Leone owes much of its importance to its deep-water harbour, which enabled maritime trade with the whole of West Africa. A short length of railway line was built to connect the Government Wharf and Water Street Station. The line was steep and winding, with a maximum gradient of one in thirty, and a minimum radius of two chains (132 feet). This image depicts one of the ubiquitous Hunslet 2-6-2 Tank Locomotives on the wharf line in Freetown, c1928.

F.A.J.Utting MA, MEd (1905-1989) Lecturer Fourah Bay College 1927-30.
Photographs donated to the Sierra Leone National Railway Museum by Joyce Chamberlain and Stanley Utting

In this image a main line train is about to leave Water Street Station, Freetown at 7.35 am, c1928. The train is hauled by SLR 4-8-0 tender locomotive No 165, built by The North British Locomotive Co in 1921.

F.A.J.Utting MA, MEd (1905-1989) Lecturer Fourah Bay College 1927-30.
Photographs donated to the Sierra Leone National Railway Museum by Joyce Chamberlain and Stanley Utting

Main line train nearing town c1927, the train is hauled by 4-8-0 tender engine No 161, built by R & W Hawthorn Leslie in 1915.

F.A.J.Utting MA, MEd (1905-1989) Lecturer Fourah Bay College 1927-30.
Photographs donated to the Sierra Leone National Railway Museum by Joyce Chamberlain and Stanley Utting

In 1926 three new Garratt Patent articulated locomotives were acquired for the SLGR. They were the first of this type to be made for a 2'6" gauge railway limited to a 5-ton axle load, and credit for their development goes to Mr. R. Malthus the then Chief Mechanical Engineer. The locomotives had four cylinders and a wheel arrangement of 2-6-2 + 2-6-2. This image depicts one of the new 'Garratt' locomotives, No51 at Bauya Junction in 1927.

F.A.J.Utting MA, MEd (1905-1989) Lecturer Fourah Bay College 1927-30.
Photographs donated to the Sierra Leone National Railway Museum by Joyce Chamberlain and Stanley Utting

In 1911, to cope with an increase in traffic, four new 2-6-2 tank engines and two 4-8-0 tender engines were purchased. Unfortunately the design of the tender engines, including No 151 depicted here, did not allow sufficient flexibility for the engines to negotiate curves at the turnouts to several station yards without derailing, so the engines stood idle until the necessary alterations to curves and sidings, at a cost of almost £2,500, could be made in 1912.

When locomotives 151 and 152, built by Nasmyth, Wilson and Co at the Bridgewater Works, Patricroft near Manchester, were eventually brought into service they hauled train loads of 132 tons and were considered to be so satisfactory that ten more of the type were acquired. Here No 151 and one of the 2-6-2 + 2-6-2 Garratts outside the sheds at Bauya Junction, c1928.

F.A.J.Utting MA, MEd (1905-1989) Lecturer Fourah Bay College 1927-30.
Photographs donated to the Sierra Leone National Railway Museum by Joyce Chamberlain and Stanley Utting

The carriage of mail was one of the most important functions of the Sierra Leone Government Railway and the railway had eight dedicated postal vehicles and received an annual subsidy for the service from the Post Office. Bauya Junction was an important stopping point for mail trains, enabling the transfer of mail between Freetown in the west, Bo to Pendembu and all places between to the east and Makeni in the north. Here, two mail trains cross over at Bauya Junction at Midday, c1927.

F.A.J.Utting MA, MEd (1905-1989) Lecturer Fourah Bay College 1927-30.
Photographs donated to the Sierra Leone National Railway Museum by Joyce Chamberlain and Stanley Utting

A total of thirty-two 2-6-2 tank engines were built for the SLGR by the Hunslet Engine Company of Leeds, between 1898 and 1954. One is seen here, hauling the local train from Freetown to Waterloo and Songo in about 1927. The picture was taken between Cline Town and Kissy.
F.A.J.Utting MA, MEd (1905-1989) Lecturer Fourah Bay College 1927-30.
Photographs donated to the Sierra Leone National Railway Museum by Joyce Chamberlain and Stanley Utting

In 1911 the railway authorities decided to move the carriage shed and District Traffic Officer's quarters to Bauya. A workshop and engine shed were constructed, and a small town developed to house the local staff. This image shows locomotive sheds at Bauya Junction, c1927. The station building can be discerned in the distance.

F.A.J.Utting MA, MEd (1905-1989) Lecturer Fourah Bay College 1927-30.
Photographs donated to the Sierra Leone National Railway Museum by Joyce Chamberlain and Stanley Utting

SLR Locomotive No 168, c1952. This locomotive was one of 37 4-8-0 tender locomotives built for the railway between 1910 and 1945, ordered from various manufacturers. No 168 was built during the 2nd World War by Andrew Barclay of Kilmarnock.

Bob Wall Collection, Sierra Leone National Railway Museum

The Sierra Leone Railway was not known for its efficient timekeeping. Here a passenger train is seen arriving 2½ hours late at Newton, just 25 miles from Freetown – a fact carefully noted by the photographer, Bob Wall.

Bob Wall Collection, Sierra Leone National Railway Museum

One of the Andrew Barclay 4-8-0 locomotives hauls a passenger train from Daru to Bo, c1952. This was one of the 4-8-0 locos converted to 0-10-0 configuration, in a not altogether successful attempt to improve their adhesion. It is reported, unsurprisingly, that they damaged the track, however several more were converted.

Bob Wall Collection, Sierra Leone National Railway Museum

Here hordes of passengers await the train arriving at Daru in 1952. As home to one of the largest military barracks in Sierra Leone, Daru was an important calling point for the railway, note the group of soldiers in uniform waiting near the station sign.

Bob Wall Collection, Sierra Leone National Railway Museum

Songo is a small community about 30 miles from Freetown by rail. Here traders are waiting on the tracks to sell their wares to passengers due to arrive on the train and schoolchildren and traders on the platform look forward to their morning journey from Songo.

Bob Wall Collection, Sierra Leone National Railway Museum

Traders from the rural hinterland regularly travelled from Songo and other rural stations to Freetown or Bo to sell their goods in the city markets. This photograph depicts Passenger train No 7 at Songo in December 1952.

Bob Wall Collection, Sierra Leone National Railway Museum

Bo is Sierra Leone's second city and the leading financial, educational and economic centre of Southern Sierra Leone. This picture was taken at Bo Station in August 1959. One of the trains is hauled by one of the new Hudswell "Enterprise" class diesels, and one of the later Barclay/ Bagnall 4-8-0 tender locos is seen on the left.

Bob Wall Collection, Sierra Leone National Railway Museum

Pendembu in Kailahun District in the eastern province of Sierra Leone lies 227½ miles from Freetown. The town is an important trading centre within reach of the borders with both Liberia and Guinea. Pendembu boasted an engine shed, a hostel for locomotive crews to enable to stay overnight before the long journey back to Bo and accommodation for local staff. This image depicts the station staff at Pendembu Station, c1952.

Bob Wall Collection, Sierra Leone National Railway Museum

Every station along the line was busy with petty traders selling their wares and crowds of market traders waiting to take their wares to the markets in Bo and Freetown. Here they are seen alongside a mixed goods train in May 1953.

Bob Wall Collection, Sierra Leone National Railway Museum

Kenema is Sierra Leone's third largest city. Its development was originally promoted by the logging and carpentry industries, which were linked to the city by the railway. Since the diamond mines were discovered in the area in 1931, Kenema has become the diamond centre of the country. This picture shows the Express at Kenema Station on 26th March 1958.

Bob Wall Collection, Sierra Leone National Railway Museum

The SLR had three officers' coaches, known as OC coaches, for the use of senior professional officers when travelling on official duty. When an officer needed to travel the coach was coupled to the rear of the train so that it could be uncoupled easily at whatever destination the Officer needed to visit. The photographer, Mr Bob Wall, was Engineer to the SLR throughout the 1950s and regularly travelled in one of the Officers' Saloons with his family when inspecting the line or working up-country. This image was taken at Bauya Junction Station with Bob's family in August 1959.

Bob Wall Collection, Sierra Leone National Railway Museum

The SLR Officers' Saloons were well-equipped inside, with everything needed for living on the move – sleeping quarters, kitchen, sitting room and bathroom. Pictured is Bob Wall's wife, Margaret.

Bob Wall Collection, Sierra Leone National Railway Museum

A special saloon was built for the private use of the Colonial Governor of Sierra Leone. The Governor's carriage was built by the Metropolitan Carriage, Wagon and Finance Co., of Birmingham in 1913. This picture of the carriage was taken in April 1960 and shows Sir Milton Margai, Chief Minister (and subsequently the first Prime minister of Sierra Leone) and Governor Sir Maurice Dorman, returning to the carriage following the opening of the new Granville deviation bridge, Kissy.

Bob Wall Collection, Sierra Leone National Railway Museum

Handcar or pump trolleys powered manually by its passengers were ideal for travelling along the line for emergency or routine track inspections. Because of their low weight and small size, they could be put on and taken off the rails at any place, allowing trains to pass. In this picture, Engineer Bob Wall and men are seen riding a hand-pumped permanent-way trolley, c1953.

Bob Wall Collection, Sierra Leone National Railway Museum

Like the pump trolleys, these lightweight self-propelled railcars, powered by internal combustion engines, were used by engineers to travel along the line. Also like the pump trolleys, in the event of a timetabled trains approaching, the railcar could be lifted off the track and then re-railed once the train had passed. Here a Wickham railcar is seen being re-railed between Songo and Mabang on 20th October 1952.

Bob Wall Collection, Sierra Leone National Railway Museum

The famous Orogu Viaduct appeared on the Sierra Leone 2s 6d postage stamp in the late 1950s. There are several versions of the spelling of this important river so throughout this book we have used the currently accepted version.

Left Here we see pedestrians using the bridge as a short cut across the raging River Orogu.
Bob Wall Collection, Sierra Leone National Railway Museum

Right A mixed passenger and goods train heads up country from Freetown and crosses Orogu Viaduct, hauled by one of the huge Garratt locomotives, c1960.
From the collection of Ziad Nassar

A passenger train to Makeni hauled by one of the newly arrived diesel locomotives crosses Orogu Viaduct in August 1959.

Bob Wall Collection, Sierra Leone National Railway Museum

Stone for ballast was quarried at Baoma, a short way north of Bo. In this picture hopper wagons, built by Robert Hudson Ltd, Gildersome, Leeds, are being loaded with stone at the Baoma quarry, c1952.

Bob Wall Collection, Sierra Leone National Railway Museum

The locomotive driver oils round SLR Garratt No 66 at Blama in October 1956. Fourteen of these very powerful locomotives were built in Manchester in the mid-1950s.

Bob Wall Collection, Sierra Leone National Railway Museum

Hunslet Engine Company SLR No 82 of 1947 takes water in January 1959.

Bob Wall Collection, Sierra Leone National Railway Museum

A batch of five 4-8-0 tender locomotives was supplied by the North British Locomotive Company in 1921. SLR No 163 is depicted here passing over the new Granville Bridge deviation, c1960.

Bob Wall Collection, Sierra Leone National Railway Museum

In 1913 approval was given for the construction of an export wharf at Fourah Bay. Preparations for the project were made with the ordering of a 60 feet overhead gantry crane, a 5-ton travelling crane and an 0-4-0 saddle tank locomotive. The plans were postponed when war broke out and eventually abandoned at the end of the hostilities. The locomotive, SLR No 10 Nellie, built by Manning Wardle in 1915 was transferred to Cline Town as yard shunter. Nellie continued in use as a shunter until the closure of the railway led to her retirement. She is depicted here at Cline Town Works in July 1958, very close to the building which now houses the National Railway Museum.

Bob Wall Collection, Sierra Leone National Railway Museum

Dieselisation started in 1954, although steam locomotives continued in traffic until closure of the railway in 1975. Eight 145HP, 20-ton 0-8-0 diesel mechanical locomotives were supplied by Hudswell-Clarke & Co Ltd of Leeds between 1958 and 1961. They were used principally for light duties and trip-working, and short distance passenger work, although they could be called on to work longer distance turns in an emergency. Here diesel No 103 is seen at Cline Town in August 1957.

Bob Wall Collection, Sierra Leone National Railway Museum

Sixteen 29-ton 2-8-2 "Enterprise Class" diesel mechanical locomotives, with Paxman Hi-Dyne engines, were also supplied by Hudswell-Clarke & Co Ltd of Leeds between 1954 and 1961. These locomotives were used for both heavy freight and long-distance passenger trains and had a maximum speed of 24 miles per hour. The first of the class was SLR No 120, which arrived by sea in July 1958.

Bob Wall Collection, Sierra Leone National Railway Museum

Here diesel No 120 is seen touching down at Queen Elizabeth Docks, Freetown in July 1958.

Bob Wall Collection, Sierra Leone National Railway Museum

On arrival in Sierra Leone diesel No 120 underwent various test runs. In this image, the locomotive is being observed by engineers on a trial train to Cline Town in July 1958.

Bob Wall Collection, Sierra Leone National Railway Museum

Whilst steam continued until the closure of the railway in the 1970s, the "Enterprise" diesels became the mainstay of the locomotive fleet. In this image diesel No 125 is seen hauling a train of Independence Coaches, at Segbwema in 1967.

Dr Peter Johnson Collection, Sierra Leone National Railway Museum

Few images remain in Sierra Leone of the period of operation between 1961 and 1975, since many of the railway's records were destroyed during the civil war of 1991 – 2002. The section through the City from Water Street to Cline Town closed first in around 1967 and all operations started at Cline Town from then until 1975. Water Street Station was retained and converted into the national bus station. Seen here from the opposite side of Water Street (now Wallace Johnson Street) in April 1975.

Pasco Rowe Collection, Sierra Leone National Railway Museum

The last General Manager of the Sierra Leone Railway, Richard Norman stands in front of Beyer-Garratt 4-8-2+2-8-4 SLR No 73 of 1955, hauling the last formal passenger train on the Sierra Leone Railway on 17th November 1974.

Pasco Rowe Collection, Sierra Leone National Railway Museum

The Pay Train continued to operate for as long as any railway line at all continued to exist and staff were employed. It finally came out of service in 1979. In this image the Pay Coach is accompanied by a travelling post office, a passenger carriage for a team of guests from the UK, and the General Manager's Coach, seen at Roponga on 30th April 1975.

R T Russell
Pasco Rowe Collection, Sierra Leone National Railway Museum

The Pay Train passes round a curve near Rotifunk on 30th April 1975.

Pasco Rowe Collection, Sierra Leone National Railway Museum

The Pay Train at Songo Station on 30th April 1975.

Pasco Rowe Collection, Sierra Leone National Railway Museum

The Pay Train at Bradford on 30th April 1975. It is hauled by Enterprise Class diesel mechanical locomotive No 123, one of the last two locomotives ever to operate on the Sierra Leone Railway.

Pasco Rowe Collection, Sierra Leone National Railway Museum

A travelling post office stands at Bauya Junction Station in April 1975.

Pasco Rowe Collection, Sierra Leone National Railway Museum

Officers' Coach No OC1291 is shunted into the consist with a travelling post office at Bauya Junction Station in April 1975.

Pasco Rowe Collection, Sierra Leone National Railway Museum

A steel bodied 8-ton Goods Brake Van stands in a line of goods vans awaiting movement at Bauya Junction Station in April 1975.

Pasco Rowe Collection, Sierra Leone National Railway Museum

SLR Enterprise Class diesel mechanical locomotive No 123 hauls a train out of Bauya Junction Station at Bauya in April 1975. The coach immediately behind the locomotive is the diesel locomotive fitter's coach. This was a former Pay Coach, converted into a mobile workshop, which went out with the locomotive to enable local repairs to be made, a sign of the notorious unreliability of the diesels.

Pasco Rowe Collection, Sierra Leone National Railway Museum

SLR train hauled by Enterprise Class diesel mechanical locomotive No 133, seen at Bauya in March 1976. By this time this locomotive had been re-engineered with a Gardner 8L3B engine and simplified transmission with a conventional Vulcan Sinclair fluid flywheel, rather than the complex Dual Fluidrive system originally fitted with a Paxman 6YHXL engine.

From the collection of Philip Cole

Goods trains were still operating as far as Bauya in March 1976, as can be seen in this picture of the yard taken from the balcony on the station building in March 1976. Note the piles of metal sleepers on the platform, awaiting transfer to Freetown as scrap.

From the collection of Philip Cole

A local makes use of a pump trolley at Bradford, April 1975.

At Cline Town Works on the outskirts of Freetown, locomotives and rolling stock awaited disposal. Here Hunslet 4-6-2 Tank Locomotive SLR No 46 sits gently rusting as it awaits the cutter's torch, April 1975.

Pasco Rowe Collection, Sierra Leone National Railway Museum

General Manager Richard Norman felt strongly that something of the railway should be kept for posterity and asked the Chief Mechanical Engineer Radcliffe Ayodele Cole to 'recommend what we can keep and what we cannot keep before we scrap the whole thing'. Among the items recommended for retention was Hudswell Clarke Diesel locomotive No 107, seen here at Cline Town in 1975.

Pasco Rowe Collection, Sierra Leone National Railway Museum

Manning Wardle 0-4-0 locomotive No 10 'Nellie' was hidden away in Cline Town Works and marked 'Not to be burnt' to ensure that she survived the torch, 16 April 1974.

Roger Darsley
Pasco Rowe Collection, Sierra Leone National Railway Museum

The large Beyer-Garratt No 73 used to haul the last passenger train was saved and placed in Cline Town Works. The General Manager Richard Norman already referred to it as a 'Museum', when this photograph was taken in January 1977.

R T Russell
Pasco Rowe Collection, Sierra Leone National Railway Museum

As Sierra Leone was being prepared for Independence in 1961, the British Government took steps to leave the railway in as good condition as possible. A fleet of 45 carriages built by the Gloucester Carriage & Wagon Co Ltd, was provided as a gift to the new government. They became known as 'Independence Coaches'. During their visit in April 1975, the team from the Welshpool & Llanfair Light Railway were able to purchase one first class and three third class carriages suitable for operation on the railway in mid-Wales. They are seen here marshalled at Cline Town awaiting transport.

Pasco Rowe Collection, Sierra Leone National Railway Museum

Hunslet 2-6-2 SLR No 85 arrives at the Welshpool & Llanfair Light Railway for the first time on August 7th, 1975.

Alan Doig
Welshpool & Llanfair Light Railway Archive

On arrival at the W&LLR No 85 was renumbered in line with the railway's numbering system and became W&LLR No 14. It is seen here in a W&LLR livery hauling two of the SLR Independence Coaches on the W&LLR in the 1980s.

Basil Roberts
Welshpool & Llanfair Light Railway Archive

The vehicles that had been retained and stored in the former carriage workshop at Cline Town Works were forgotten about during the bloody rebel war between 1991 to 2002. The Works became a refuge for some ten thousand displaced people who fled to Freetown from the Provinces and the locomotives and carriages hidden there were stripped of fittings and panelling.

In September 2004, Colonel Steve Davies MBE arrived in Sierra Leone on military service and, being a railway enthusiast, quickly began to explore the remains of the former railway. On a visit to Cline Town on Saturday 18th September 2004 he re-discovered the collection and was able to bring it to the attention of the President of the Republic of Sierra Leone, Alhaji Dr Ahmad Tejan Kabbah. The President supported the idea of developing a national museum on the site and gave Colonel Davies the authority to do so.

On discovering the collection hidden away in the carriage works building, Colonel Steve Davies MBE was introduced to the former Works Manager, Mohamed Momodu Bangura, a lifelong railway engineer who was able to explain the background to each vehicle. Mohamed is pictured here with Manning Wardle 0-4-0ST SLR No 10 'Nellie' on Sunday 19th September 2004.

Steve Davies MBE

Peering through the windows of the works on that very first visit Colonel Davies had been astounded to see a huge steam locomotive looming through the gloom. It turned out to be the Beyer-Garratt 4-8-2+2-8-4 SLR No 73, which had hauled the last passenger train back in 1975. Most of the non-ferrous fittings had been stolen, but the motion was completely intact and the platework in very good condition.

Steve Davies MBE

At the back of the building, Hudswell Clarke Diesel locomotive No 107 and Hunslet 2-4-2T No 81 sat, draped in cobwebs and dust. Colonel Davies noted that No 107 was in reasonable condition, but some engine parts and radiator were missing. No 81 was in poor condition but platework sound and cosmetically restorable.

Steve Davies MBE

In front of No 107 stood the two last diesel locomotives to have operated on the SLR: Hudswell Clarke Enterprise Class diesel mechanical locomotives No 123 and 133.

No 123 was fitted with a Paxman V-6 diesel engine which was missing the cylinder head block and various non-ferrous components, but the bodywork was in good condition underneath the grime. No 133 was fitted with a virtually complete Gardner 8-in-line diesel. The gearbox and final drives were all intact. The locomotive was in good overall condition and the cab fittings were virtually complete.

Steve Davies MBE

On the opposite side of the building stood the only surviving goods vehicle, the diesel locomotive fitters' coach and a Wickham inspection trolley No 9534, built in May 1964. The bodies of both vehicles were in reasonable condition, but the internal components had been stripped.

Steve Davies MBE

In front of the Wickham inspection trolley stood Hudswell Clarke diesel locomotive No 105, sister engine to 107. Colonel Davies noted that the locomotive was virtually intact, but some key components were missing. He felt that the locomotive could possibly provide donor parts for 107 to make one complete engine.

Steve Davies MBE

This vehicle had been completely stripped of its rolled steel panelling and internal fittings, but Mohamed Bangura was rightly proud of the vehicle. It was the remains of a special carriage built at Cline Town Works for the visit of H.M. Queen Elizabeth II in November 1961 to celebrate the independence of Sierra Leone. Unfortunately, the itinerary for the royal visit was changed at the last minute and Her Majesty never got to travel in the coach.

Steve Davies MBE

These two former Officers' Coaches had also been completely stripped, with one of the surviving body frames showing considerable decay. The decision was taken to scrap the one in worst condition and to use the components to help refurbish the remaining vehicle. This carriage is built on Gibbins spring frame bogies suggesting it was built by Gloucester Carriage and Wagon Works or converted from a vehicle built by them.

Steve Davies MBE

Two of the steel-bodied 1961 'Independence' coaches had survived, Private & Officer's Coach No 3 and a third-class passenger carriage. Both had been internally stripped, and the distinctive large springs had been stolen, it was not possible to move the vehicles from their existing position.

Steve Davies MBE

The Governor's Coach had been preserved, and although the interior had been gutted some of the original panelling and marquetry has survived. The British coat of arms on the balcony end of the vehicle had been replaced with the Sierra Leone National Arms.

Steve Davies MBE

The Pay Coach was certainly sufficiently important to be preserved and was found in very good condition, not requiring much more than a good clean and a repaint to make it fit for display.

Steve Davies MBE

At the far corner of the building was found 13-ton bogie goods wagon built by G.R. Turner of Langley Mill, Nottinghamshire. Literally hundreds of these general-purpose goods vehicles provided the means by which many farmers, producers and manufacturers got their wares to market. They were critical to the supply of fresh produce for Freetown, and it is said that major markets were closed to many producers when the railway closed. The roads were simply not up to the job of providing an efficient alternative to the train. We believe this to be the last surviving such goods wagon in the entire country and it has remained in excellent condition.

Steve Davies MBE

The first task in developing the museum was to recruit a team of local men to form a restoration team who would clean, repair and restore the collection to an acceptable standard for conservation and display.

Steve Davies MBE

Cosmetic restoration of the collection started in September 2004, with the fourteen new recruits learning how to rub down metal and wooden surfaces, carry out basic repair work, paint, line and letter the vehicles. Here No 81 is being rubbed down by Santigi Konteh in preparation for repainting.

Steve Davies MBE

The Restoration team worked in groups cleaning several vehicles at once. Here they are seen cleaning and rubbing down No 123, No 133 and the Garratt, under the eagle eye of Colonel Davies.

Steve Davies MBE

You can really see the difference in this photograph of the two Enterprise Class diesels and the Garratt, as the team have cleaned away the years of residual rust and dirt. The inspection pits had by now been cleared of vast quantities of accumulated debris.

Steve Davies MBE

It was not practical to acquire rolled steel in Sierra Leone to replace the sheeting stolen from the body of the Queen's Coach, and so the coach bodied was recreated using marine ply. The cosmetic appearance is now just as it was in 1961.

Steve Davies MBE

The available options for paint are limited in Sierra Leone and therefore it is sometimes difficult to recreate exact liveries. The Garratt was delivered in Gorton green and so the nearest available match was acquired.

Steve Davies MBE

In March 2005 Colonel Davies was by now 6 months into his 14-month tour of duty in Sierra Leone. Although there was still work to be done on the development of the museum, this seemed like an appropriate time to have a test opening. Amidst a crowd of invited dignitaries including the President of the Republic of Sierra Leone Alhaji Dr Ahmad Tejan Kabbah and Director of the National Railway Museum, York, Mr Andrew Scott CBE the museum was officially launched. Here the invited guests stand during the Sierra Leone National Anthem. On the left is President Kabbah and to his right is Andrew Scott CBE.

Steve Davies MBE

Colonel Davies gave the President a guided tour of the museum.

Steve Davies MBE

Andrew Scott CBE was delighted to pose with a former locomotive driver in the cab of Enterprise Class diesel locomotive No 133.

Steve Davies MBE

The Restoration Team posed, in their brand-new boiler suits, with Colonel Davies and the President to celebrate their huge achievements.
Steve Davies MBE

Once the formalities were over the general public were invited to come into the museum and to see what was being developed there. The curiosity of local people was enormous and many of them had never seen a museum before, but all were amazed to see the collection that had been hidden there for thirty years.

Steve Davies MBE

Conservation of the collections is continual since the climate in Sierra Leone is hostile to the preservation of wood and paint, with extremes of heat and a seasonal swing between very low and very high humidity. Repainting takes place regularly and work is gradually taking place to restore the interiors of the carriages or at least make them presentable for access, with special exhibitions inside. Here we see the Bayer Garratt No 73 after a recent repaint in 2016.

William Bickers-Jones

Hunslet 2-6-2T No 81 is kept clean and tidy pending further restoration work. Seen here in 2016.

William Bickers-Jones

In November 2018, Welshpool & Llanfair Light Railway member Simon Bowden carried out further cosmetic work on No 81, cleaning off and repainting a surviving worksplate, the regulator handle and various other components.

Author

Manning Wardle 0-4-0 locomotive SLR No 10 'Nellie' had been painted black in the latter years of operation and repainted in the same livery in the original cosmetic restoration. Having discovered the original specification in the Hunslet Archive in the UK, the locomotive was repainted in Manning Wardle's standard livery of brown with black and yellow lining in March 2016.

It has subsequently been further improved by the addition of new replica name and worksplates, kindly sponsored by Michael Whitehouse.

Adrian Ashby

Hudswell Clarke diesel locomotive No 105 is equally clean and in excellent cosmetic condition. Pictured here in March 2016.

William Bickers-Jones

The Queen's Coach requires particular attention, since the dusty climate destroys the white paint quite rapidly. The coach has been repainted every two to three years since the museum opened to keep it in good condition and to protect the wood from rotting.

William Bickers-Jones

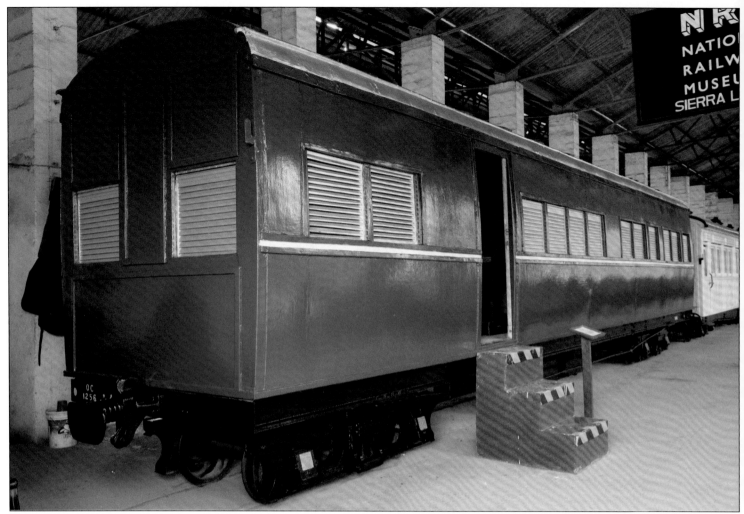

The General Manager's Coach was substantially rebuilt using marine ply for the bodywork. In 2018 the interior was painted out and an exhibition of photographs relating to the story of the Officer's Coaches installed.

William Bickers-Jones

Like the Queen's Coach, the Governor's Coach is repainted every two to three years. A display about the coach has been installed inside and plans are being developed to do a full restoration of the interior when resources permit.

William Bickers-Jones

In 2019 the two Independence Coaches were repainted for the first time since the museum opened. Depicted here in October 2019 having the lettering restored.

Author

The diesel fitters' coach remains in good cosmetic condition as it is at the rear of the museum with less exposure to light and dirt than many of the vehicles. The coach has not required repainting but lettering on the side of the vehicle was replaced in November 2019.

William Bickers-Jones

Like the diesel fitters' coach, the Pay Coach shows no sign of deterioration and is good candidate for the development of a future internal display about the role of the Pay Train.

William Bickers-Jones

The Wickham Inspection Trolley underwent further cosmetic restoration in 2017. The missing trapdoor in the floor was replaced and the vehicle was repainted inside and out. It was further enhanced by simulating the original glass panel in the front of the vehicle, by painting the metal panel silver and by the addition of appropriate headlights.

Author

The Goods Van was painted with aluminium paint and lining and lettering replaced in 2018 as part of a training programme for the current museum staff.

Author

Another important aspect of museum work is to survey the remains of the railway that are still in situ and, working with the Monuments & Relics Commission (the government agency responsible for the museum), to agree the best course of action for preservation. The old station at Newton is located in the grounds of Amadiyya Secondary School and was in dilapidated condition. However, it was agreed that the best solution would be to preserve the station and its sign in situ.

Abdul Karim Kamara

The museum team have visited Newton Station to carry out a cleaning exercise in the surrounding area and to repaint the station sign. This will be accompanied by an educational programme and the development of a school Heritage Club where the pupils will learn about their heritage and carry out associated conservation projects.

Abdul Karim Kamara

A trip up-country in November 2019 revealed a number of station signs that were at risk of destruction, through building encroachment or environmental damage. In discussions with the Deputy Minister of Tourism & Cultural Affairs and local chiefs, in May 2020 three signs were removed from their original locations and brought to the museum for safekeeping.

Abdul Karim Kamara

The signs from Segbwema, Hangha and Blama have now been re-erected on public display in the museum compound.

Abdul Karim Kamara

On Tuesday 10th March 2020 a special programme took place at Bauya Junction Station, presided over by the Hon Deputy Minister of Tourism & Cultural Affairs and chaired by the Director of Culture, Ministry of Tourism & Cultural Affairs, to celebrate the declaration of the site as protected cultural property.

Author

The programme was attended by the local community and invited guests and included local traditional dancing, speeches and presentations by local and national dignitaries. A school heritage club was formed of pupils from St Peter's Secondary School, who performed a skit charting the history of the railway. Members of the heritage club pose by the original station sign at Bauya on 10th March 2020.

Author

The Sierra Leone National Railway Museum is much more than simply a repository for railway artefacts, but an important cultural and social centre. It boasts a rich and vibrant educational programme attracting school groups at all levels.

In March 2020 over 100 pupils form Henmat International Elementary School, Freetown enjoyed learning the Bo Train Song, riding the pump trolley and colouring in railway pictures.

Author

The Islamic Federation School of Freetown enjoyed a guided tour of the museum with Senior Tour Guide, Mohamed Jabbie in October 2016.

Author

The most popular exhibit with school children is the pump trolley. This "SF handcar" pump trolley was manufactured by D Wickham & Co. of Ware, Hertfordshire, England and originally worked in Bo.

Author

The adult education and community programme is equally important to the museum, which is now the only public facility in the eastern end of Freetown. In October 2019 the local Sowei Women's Society had a special programme in support of the campaign against child initiation in Bondo (FGM).

Author

On March 12th, 2020 the Sierra Leone National Railway Museum celebrated its 15th anniversary. A special 15th anniversary programme at the National Railway Museum was attended by representatives of local businesses, the local community, schools, dignitaries from a broad range of Freetown institutions and ministries, the British High Commissioner, our UK visitors and representatives of the Ministry of Tourism & Cultural Affairs. Here Mr Abu Bakarr Nylander-Kargbo, Museum Coordinator, gives a vote of thanks to invited guests and speakers at the end of the ceremony.

Author

Part of the 15th Anniversary celebrations included a formal twinning ceremony between the Sierra Leone National Railway Museum and the Welshpool & Llanfair Light Railway. In this photograph, the Honourable Deputy Minister of Tourism & Cultural Affairs, Mr William I K Robinson, exchanges commemorative plaques with Mr Steve Clews, Chairman of the W&LLR. The plaque presented by the W&LLR is made using an original works plate from Hunslet 2-6-2 locomotive SLR No 84 which had been found in store at the railway.

Author

FRIENDS OF THE
SIERRA LEONE
NATIONAL RAILWAY MUSEUM

JOIN US ON OUR INCREDIBLE JOURNEY

JOIN TODAY AND GET ALL THIS!

Quarterly newsletters
Opportunities to visit Freetown and go on expeditions &
adventures with the UK team of experts and curators

www.SierraLeoneRailwayMuseum.com
foslnrm@outlook.com

I ♥
NATIONAL
RAILWAY
MUSEUM